a touring exhibition organised by
The South Bank Centre and the
Laing Art Gallery, Newcastle upon Tyne

The Experience of Painting

EIGHT MODERN ARTISTS

Gillian Ayres
Francis Davison
Jennifer Durrant
James Hugonin
Albert Irvin
Edwina Leapman
Kenneth Martin
Bridget Riley

THE SOUTH BANK CENTRE

PREFACE

In mounting *The Experience of Painting* we have sought to show something of the great variety and quality of abstract, or non-representational, painting made in this country in recent years. The exhibition presents in some depth the work of seven painters and one collagist, who taken collectively, have sustained many decades of consistent and fertile activity. It also attempts to give the visitor an insight into the working practice of each artist.

We are grateful to the artists, their galleries, and other lenders who have enthusiastically responded to our project. The six living artists and Margaret Mellis, widow of Francis Davison, have generously and patiently coped with our requests for interviews, photographs and other information.

This catalogue – its introduction and the texts deriving from interviews – is the work of the writer and teacher Mel Gooding. With sensitivity, persistence and understanding he has carried through a task, the scale and difficulty of which no-one quite foresaw.

Finally, we have been delighted to work with Mike Collier, Senior Art Exhibition Officer at the Laing Art Gallery in Newcastle. From the first coincidence of ideas we have enjoyed what we trust has been a worthwhile and fruitful collaboration.

Joanna Drew
Director of the Hayward Gallery and Regional Exhibitions

Michael Harrison
Assistant Director for Regional Exhibitions

The Experience of Painting

NOTES AND VOICES
AN INTRODUCTION TO THE EXHIBITION

New orientations are first mirrored in art. It will be so again: a new poetry will be extracted from vision.

ADRIAN STOKES

In order to understand the true meaning of Abstract Art, we have to conceive of ourselves as a reflex (reflection) of reality. This means we have to see ourselves as a mirror in which reality reflects itself.

PIET MONDRIAN

I

Before we speak of the experience of painting let us consider our experience of the world. We exist in space, at this moment in time; but how little that says of our condition! This instant is one of innumerable successive such moments in our existence; we bring to it both memory and anticipation, the double-edged consciousness of what is lost and what is potential, what has passed and what is to come. Memories, dreams, desires, our imaginings of history, our projections of futurity, our sense of what is true and what is false, all converge upon this moment, as we stand, say, upon a beach, and looking seawards, smell the salt upon the air, feel the wind cold on our cheek.

"The business of art is to reveal the relation between man and his circumambient universe, at the living moment."

D. H. LAWRENCE

We are subject to everything that is happening externally in that particular moment, the air, the wind, the sand, the pebbles, the sea, the spray, the birds. We look, and take everything in at one go, see it as a whole. And then our eye focusses upon a particular, an object or a pattern in things, a seagull or the play of a wave, and simultaneously our ear may seek to isolate a sound that differentiates itself from the general tumult. And so it goes on, this constant shifting between our apprehension of the thing as a whole and our perception of the parts that make up the whole, between picking out the detail and composing the unity. Any picture of the scene, silent and static, will necessarily abstract from the reality, and present us only with aspects of it. Even moments of calm in nature are actually made up of thousands of minute modulations and changes, modulations of light and shade, the flicker of nature. There is never a moment of absolute stillness in nature.

Art may reflect something of this evanescence, but its purposes are deeper than a mirroring of the actual. It is an *imaginative and metaphorical* interaction with the world and its objects, answering to the deepest human impulse: to find meaning in the flux, to structure coherences, to express a truth about the underlying patterns in things; patterns that may be revealed only by creative human intervention. It shares these purposes with science and philosophy at their most disinterested, but it has a spiritual autonomy that those pursuits lack, for it is not susceptible to utility. Its discovery of the real, in terms of image and form, is what gives art its vitality, its living quality: that inherent power to move us, and to increase our sense of what it is to be alive, to be in vital relation to the world we live in. Such a relation must accommodate what art reveals, the inescapable transcience of things. All art reminds us of our mortality. All art is concerned with what may counter that realisation.

. . . . If by eternity is understood not endless temporal duration but timelessness, then he lives eternally who lives in the present. Our life is endless in the way that our visual field is without limit.

LUDWIG WITTGENSTEIN

(The artist) does not attach such intense importance to natural form as do many realist critics, because, for him, these final forms are not the real stuff of the process of natural creation. For he places more value on the powers which do the forming than on the final forms themselves. . . . . Thus he surveys with a penetrating eye the finished forms which nature places in front of him. . . . The deeper he looks, the more readily he can extend his view from present to past, the more deeply he is impressed by the one essential image of creation itself, as Genesis, rather than by the image of nature, the finished product. . . . Then he permits himself the thought that the process of creation can today hardly be complete and he sees the act of world creation stretching from the past to the future. Genesis eternal!

PAUL KLEE

II

There is a great deal more to the business of looking at the world than is implied by the notion of "picturing", the act of composing a view. We do not perceive the world around us, and through which we move, as a picture or as a series of pictures. We do not perceive the space we inhabit as it was imagined and constructed by the great theoreticians and practitioners of mathematical and aerial perspective: we do not view it as from a fixed viewpoint through a window. Neither do we see things with the still sharpness of focus with which they are reflected in the mirrors of a *camera obscura*, that other great invention of Renaissance naturalism. In short, our space is not framed by the conventional devices that determine the picturing of natural facts in representational painting. Our apprehension of the world is at once more complex, and more direct; we experience the cosmos as from its centre.

Following poets and metaphysicians (and also Van Gogh, who said "Life is probably *round*.") the French phenomenologist Gaston Bachelard wrote: "The world is round around the round being." We experience Bachelard's "roundness of the world" as simultaneous light, temperature and space; we are enveloped by it; it is our complex element. Within its multidimensional space, stretching away before us, arching (metaphorically) above us, surrounding us, we encounter its multifarious objects, given colour and form by light and shadow. Our vision adjusts its focus continuously, seeing now in clarity the objects in its foreground, now those at a distance, becoming aware, out of the corner of our eye, of those to this side or that, which by turning our head we bring into full view. Our visual apprehension of the world is dynamic; as we change, everything else changes, as we move through space every relation shifts; this complex actuality no picture can capture.

" – Finally I must tell you that as a painter I am becoming more clear sighted before nature, but that with me the realisation of my sensations is always painful. I cannot attain the intensity that is unfolded before my senses. I have not the magnificent richness of colouring that animates nature. Here on the bank of the river the motifs multiply, the same subject seen from a different angle often subject for study of the most powerful interest and so varied that I think I could occupy myself for months without changing place, by turning now more to the right, now more to the left."
                                                                                                                    PAUL CEZANNE

"The world is everything that is the case" Wittgenstein said. For a start, it is what presents itself to us as sight and sound, touch, smell and taste. But it is more than the sum of the facts simultaneously experienced through those senses. What is also the case is the *imagination* that we bring to the perceived world, that shaping faculty empowered not only by our experience not only of external actualities, but also by our developing intelligence and understanding, and our emotions. Out of an infinitude of possibilities there is differentiated that coherence which we call our *reality*: this is the outcome of innumerable acts of intuitive perception, of insight into the relations between things, and of the constructive, or creative, process of deciphering, or construing, the actual world.

Let us clarify the distinction. What is *actual* is what may be said to exist, whether we recognise its existence or not (and there are whole worlds hidden from our ordinary senses, that have been revealed by slow motion and high-speed photography, astronomy and microscopy). What is *real* is what *we make* of what exists, as we encounter it, in the act of recognition, of the knowing of something in such a way *that we may know it again*. There are many ways of knowing, means to recognition, physical and metaphysical; there are many levels of reality. Art is a means to knowledge, to a discovery of the real.

Appearances reach us through the eye, and the eye – whether we speak with the psychologist or the embryologist – is part of the brain and therefore hopelessly involved in mysterious cerebral operations. Thus nature presents every generation (and every person who will use his eyes for more than nodding recognitions) with a unique and unrepeated facet of appearance. And the Ineluctable Modality of the Visible – young Dedalus' hypnotic phrase – is a myth that evaporates between any two works of representation. . . . And if appearances are thus unstable in the human eye, their representation in art is not a matter of mechanical reproduction but of progressive revelation.
                                                                                                                    LEO STEINBERG

Each of the artists in this exhibition is concerned with the revelation of reality. They all speak, with differences of emphasis and preoccupation, about the relation of their work to the perceived world. Each of them is engaged in a process of transformation. Through their premeditated action upon specific materials, that which enters their subjective consciousness through the senses is transmuted into an object having expressive force, what Suzanne Langer called "vital import." They speak of the ways in which their work treats of the phenomenal, of its dealings with light and space, and with the forms that are revealed and defined in space by light and colour. Those things are the very substance of their art itself, and in speaking of them they call attention to the *objective autonomy of the work*, and of its hard-won freedom from the hopeless task of imitating or describing outward appearances in terms of outworn conventions.

And I know that World Is a World of Imagination and Vision. I see Everything I paint In This World, but

Every body does not see alike. To the Eyes of the Miser a Guinea is more beautiful than the Sun, and a bag worn with the use of Money has more beautiful proportions than a Vine filled with Grapes. The tree which moves some to tears of joy is in the eyes of others only a Green thing that stands in the way. Some see Nature all Ridicule and Deformity, and by these I shall not regulate my proportions; and Some Scarce see Nature at all. But to the Eyes of the Man of Imagination, Nature is Imagination itself. As a man is, So he Sees. As the eye is formed, such are its Powers. WILLIAM BLAKE

III

None of the artists in this exhibition deploys a symbolism in the sense of something pictured which may stand for something quite other, as an object may stand for a quality for instance (a candle for transience, a book for learning) or a sign for an idea (as a cross may represent Christianity, a crown, kingship). But in the most fundamental sense all the works in this exhibition are symbolic objects. They transform some aspect of lived experience, some feeling, some sense of things, conscious or unconscious, inner or outward, into a sign. That sign is, however, something other than a conventional indicator. It is complex and indeterminate in its effects: what is expressed, or carried, by the object that confronts us is not translatable, it can only be apprehended by the viewer, looking at the work. For what it treats of is inaccessible to both ordinary language and logical discourse, and what it reveals, its true subject, can be represented *only in visual terms*, and in the form it has found. "A painting has to exude more than an effect" wrote Mark Tobey. "Man's true world is his thought and his thought is reflected in his art as well as in everything else he does."

For this reason it is fascinating, and helpful, to hear from the artists themselves how these works are made. For all their differences, it is clear from their descriptions of their practice that each of these artists works in ways that can only be described as intuitive and explorative: they work without specific communicative intention towards the *discovery* of the image; they cannot know when they begin where they will end. Art comes in the knowing when they have found the image; in the mastery of the media and of the technical processes that make exploration possible; and in the patient and often monotonous procedures that lead up to the moment of discovery, the moment when reality is revealed.

There is nothing in nature that is not in us.
Whatever exists in nature, exists in us in the form of our awareness of its existence. All creative activities of Mankind consist in the search for an expression of that awareness.
The perceptible results of that creative search are the so-called fact-findings of science, the conceptions and ideas of philosophy, the inventions in technics and the images of the visual arts. NAUM GABO

MEL GOODING November 1988

A NOTE ON THE TEXTS

With two exceptions, the texts which follow are the outcome of conversations I recorded with the artists in the Autumn of this year. Transcripts, and notes taken at the time, provided the basis for an editing which eliminated my own spoken contribution, and which sought to bring out the essence of what the artist had actually said about some of the issues over which our talk ranged. There were no prepared questions, and consequently no premeditated answers, no rehearsed "statements". I was helped by further talk with the artists after my preparation of a draft text.

For particular emphases of subject matter I must take editorial responsibility, although in every case I was concerned above all to reflect in the text the particular and special preoccupations of the individual artist. It would have defeated my purpose entirely to have abstracted only those things which in some way matched or confirmed any preconceptions I may have had. It is one of the joys of conversation that it is open and divergent; it leads us into paths we had not known to be there; we surprise ourselves, with invention and discovery.

The reader should expect, therefore, the occasional inconsistency in what an artist says, or the apparent contradictions in these texts: it is in the nature of conversation to be exploratory and provisional or tentative in its formulations. Contradiction and inconsistency are virtues of the unrehearsed spoken word; they reflect the true nature of thought about difficult things in which terms are not agreed: they are part of the way in which truth is negotiated out of a shared desire to catch it. It is possible anyway to say one thing at one time and something quite different at another, *and to mean both*.

In any case it was not to my purpose in editing these conversations to tidy up or falsely construct a logical coherence out of generously unguarded utterance. It was my aim to catch the tone and the genuine mode of the artist's way of speaking about their work, and in this way to share something of the pleasure that I have enjoyed in their company and conversation.

This meant keeping in repetition and emphasis, and retaining the mode of direct address, that personal and sometimes emphatic way of speaking which seeks an affirmative response, the nod of agreement or of understanding from the interlocutor. I think in this way these texts come closer than written formulations usually do to the true uncertainties and genuine perplexities that often attend upon an artist's thinking about his or her work, and to the honest diffidences that are characteristic of most artists' utterance on the subject. To have some insight into these things can only increase our admiration for the courage and determination of the artist's single-minded pursuit, *in the making of the work*, of truth and beauty. And it will surely serve to encourage the spectator to put aside prejudice, and to come to the work in a receptive generosity of spirit, prepared to be surprised by delight, and moved to new ways of seeing.

Of the two exceptional texts, that on the work of Francis Davison was made after conversations with Margaret Mellis, the artist's widow, and that of Kenneth Martin's was constructed from his own writings.

Those who remember the astounding revelation of the exhibition of Francis Davison's work organised at the Hayward Gallery by Julian Spalding in 1982 will recall the complete and disconcerting absence of any personal details of the artist, of any information about his work and its development, even of titles and dates of composition. Davison maintained a notable and rigorously principled silence about his work: *it was what it was*, and not something else; he was not interested in the manoeuvres of art historians, who often seem to be interested in everything else *but* the work itself. (I am reminded of the American artist Ad Reinhardt's *Art-as-Art dogma*: "The one thing to say about art is that it is one thing. Art is art-as-art and everything else is everything else. Art-as-art is nothing but art. Art is not what is not art."

The text that is the outcome of my conversation with Margaret Mellis throws light upon Davison's work without transgressing his principles: it directs our attention to the work itself, it resists irrelevant or sentimental musings. Its insights derive from her intense closeness to the work, and her knowledge of its making is that of a fellow artist and exemplary companion in the virtually hidden adventure of his creative life.

Kenneth Martin wrote and spoke with great clarity of insight into his own creative processes; he was capable of both technical exposition and of eloquent testimony to the relation of his art to life. I felt it appropriate to draw upon the extensive body of his writings and lectures to create a text which would represent truly and aptly his ideas and beliefs, which developed within a framework of remarkable consistency.

In each of these cases the rationale was in keeping with that underlying the construction of all these texts: *to enable the reader to hear the authentic voice of the speaker.*

Mel Gooding November 1988

GILLIAN AYRES

Making
the
work

However I start the paintings, it's not necessarily how I'll go on with them. I may start with my hands; I do actually think that the hands and fingers are very sensitive instruments for painting. I don't mean I just apply great handfuls of paint, though I may do that. And then I may use a brush; in some parts of a painting the touch may be very fine. It's a process of looking for something to happen in the painting. You want to paint the paintings that you would like to see, but you don't always manage to do it.

I can feel happy about a painting when I have just done it, and find that when I come back to it next morning I don't feel happy at all. I have had paintings around the studio and I have certainly felt they were finished, and then next week or whenever I have wanted to work on them again. That is how the paintings get thick; that thickness of working has nothing to do with ambition, it's just that one has gone on with them, sometimes for years.

There's nothing doctrinaire in my approach: I have no idea how things *should* be done. There are no ethics to it. I have an idea that the paintings go on from each other; you do a spate of work, and the last one affects the next, and then you might go back again and work on the previous one again. You are simply evolving something, rather in the way perhaps that a bar of music or a line of poetry follows on from the last, developing and changing. It's not a matter of chance, but you can have good days and bad days, and I'm not able to explain that: it's like in tennis, you know you can suddenly sense that you are going to make a shot better than you usually do, and you do, and then you can't do it again. Sometimes you are on form and sometimes not, but what is it? I don't know what this thing is, but *I know* it happens in making paintings.

Another thing is that I *look* for longer than I paint. I might work very hard for half an hour, and then get back from the painting and simply look at it, and this can go on for a long time. I mean I have no idea how much one sits back and looks.

Scale

I'm not concerned with the large scale as a means to be imposing, or to make people notice. Those things never come into it. I love a certain sort of scale: from nine by nine to about nine by twelve; it's a human scale, one that relates to the body. I use a ladder, which is really just like an extension of myself, and that size has to do really with the scale of an arm movement: it's to do with my own size, and myself against that sort of scale. There's an element of ambition to it as well: I'm not saying I get it, but I sense that you can *aim* for a sort of sublime; it gives you that possibility. That's not something you can get looking into a one by one foot canvas, or a Persian miniature, say, however exquisite.

The eighteenth century sublime was concerned with the effect of nature. An artist like Turner was concerned with the plastic things in nature – clouds, wind and rain, steam, sea, cliffs, as parallels with the plastic things in paint. James Ward's *Gordale Scar* isn't a great painting but it is a wonderful painting nevertheless, and I always go and look at it when I'm bored or fed up at the Tate; and then at the same time I'll go and look at the Morris Louis: they're two very different paintings but they've both got something of that quality of the sublime. To get something of that quality, of the grand things in nature, but to make the paint *itself* do it, has been a constant ambition; one's looking for something like that to happen.

James Ward *Gordale Scar* 1812-15
Tate Gallery, London

Fairest of Stars 1984

A Painted Tale 1985

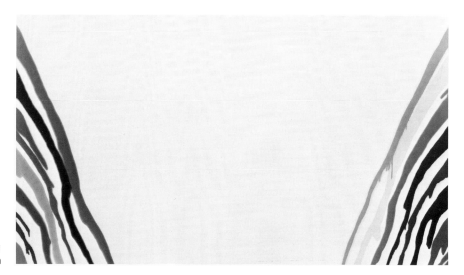

Morris Louis *Alpha-Phi* 1961
Tate Gallery, London

Any work of art has its own terms, which are certain rhythms and patterns. Every brush mark adds up to a certain surface, and to a lot of other things obviously; it adds up to shape, which adds up to scale, and within an area it adds up to a composition. But especially it adds up to *surface*. And that will have a certain style, and style is something you can't help; whatever your intentions, it is recognisable like people's handwriting: really, it is all *drawing*.

Colour The colour I use doesn't come from nature in any direct sort of way. *It comes from pots of paint.* And that is very true. I can feel very excited by paint, I always have done; even buying paint, different paints for different colours. I don't like painting if I haven't got lots of colours.

I don't like that sort of dirtying up and toning down which has been so often characteristic of painting in this country; or the way in which the black in a drawing is translated into a dark tone in a painting, and the white into light. In fact a black line or dark shape can become a yellow mark or area in a painting, it can become a matter of *intensity* rather than of *tone*. I naturally respond to tactile painting and painting that is about colour. It is very obvious in French painting, and in French drawing: Bonnard's black and white drawings, for instance, have something of the clarity of French colourism. Of course Venetian painting has this quality as well, and so do Persian miniatures. I like the dynamics that occur between complementaries. Rather than tone, I want to use the colour in a painting to give it its visual weight.

Painting and reality I think art is a lovely, indulgent, *enjoyable* thing; I don't think one has to apologise, or explain anything to anyone. All my life I have looked, listened, read: that has been my great pleasure, with other people: that is what it is all about. I'm speaking here about enjoying other people's art. *Making* art itself can be a very different thing: it's not all like a jolly Ken Russell film. It's not so much fun when the bloody thing doesn't come off. It would be nice to think that my paintings might just give delight. I'm a simple soul like that. If someone says of the work that it's horrid, I feel sad; if someone says its nice, I feel happy. I mean *anybody*; there is no great authority of opinion. There is a mainstream, but that is sorted out by time.

When one was younger one was in a minority in this country being an abstract painter; this is not the case now. As far as the visual arts were concerned this country after the war was a backwater compared to what was going on elsewhere. I think one felt passionately that we didn't see enough; we were always looking for something that we hadn't seen before.

Abstract art has been the absolute force in visual art in this century. This has nothing to do with myself, and my own commitment to abstraction. Modernism meant a lot of different things, and some of those things one may not like or agree with. But what it meant above all was hope in a brave new world. And what did go on under Modernism was *a questioning and thinking*. In fact the whole of Western society since the Renaissance has been a society that moves and questions. I don't quite see that clear cut between the pre-modern and the modern that some earlier artists did. In fact I can see modern art coming for a very long time. And under Modernism, that questioning is almost a condition of being creative.

We all want truth; that is reality. Art gets there in the form of poetic or artistic truths, which are products of the creative imagination. That's what is behind it all, and it means you want to shock yourself a bit, make something new. You could simply say that the imagination is *anti-cliché, against known experience*. You are always trying to find something you haven't seen before, an experience that is true to oneself.

Barnes   October 1988

FRANCIS DAVISON

from a conversation with Margaret Mellis

The reality of art

Francis was reluctant to title his works, or to date or classify them in any way, because he wanted you to look at the *collage* itself, without any preconceived ideas which might have been suggested by the title. In exactly the same way he felt that dates were irrelevant. People always look at those other things first, the things round the edge, title and date and so on; and that stops them seeing the work itself.

In the earlier paintings and *collages*, there is sometimes a reference to things in the world, a house and a hill, or a road perhaps, but even then he turned those houses or hills into shapes that work together, they are not houses, they are shapes, *but we read them as houses*. So it is not much of a step from representation to non-representation.

I have had to invent all the titles, so that you know which *collage* you are talking about. Simply numbering them gets too complicated; they don't correspond with numbers in catalogues and so on. The one called *Garden* is unusual because the title might direct your attention in some way. It was made for a competition which had a garden theme. This *collage* gives you a feeling of trellises and flowers, and it is a perfectly beautiful colour. It might correspond in some way to something you have experienced in the world but it is not the same thing; and if it has a good enough structure and colour it doesn't matter what *you* might think it is, because the work is stronger than anyone's thoughts.

Francis wasn't trying to do anything for the viewer. He was dealing with his own experience. When his inner feelings have *become* the material, that is where the satisfaction lies. So these *collages* present us with something that is nearer to our true experience of the world than a picture of something which can only present one aspect of it. I think that is why painters move from representation to abstraction, because it gives them greater scope and freedom, and helps them to avoid being cluttered up with pre-conceived ideas. Art is more than a matter of emotions, it is perceptual, and conceptual; it is many things simultaneously.

Making the work

The medium of *collage* gave Francis tremendous freedom, and it worked for him because of his very strong sense of structure and design. The way he approached it meant that he was able to work with the total surface the whole time. There was nothing precisely preconceived in this manner of working: it was a process of spontaneous discovery that would go on until the work was made. At the end, everything looked right, the right coloured shape in the right place.

Francis always said he was the only true *collagist*, because other people painted their paper, or put other things in, things that had other associations. He didn't put anything extra in. He just worked with these used papers. They had to be *used* papers, they couldn't be anything else.

Chance and intention

Francis's work was both completely spontaneous and controlled, two opposite things. There is always more than one thing happening at once; which is why they are interesting.

Flashing light and dark colours c.1978-83

Crossed Paths 1978-81

Black Landscape c.1952-1960
63.5 x 74.9 (not in exhibition)

18

Some people might think that there was a great deal of chance and accident in the making of the work, but there aren't any accidents in it at all. *There is nothing there that is not intended*. Say you put a piece of blue on here, or green, and it isn't right, it doesn't work, you take it off again, until you find the right shaped colour. And that is not chance. It is a matter of judgement and intention.

I used to think that there were a lot of chance things which happened to come right because of the rhythm of the working as it were. But when Francis was half-paralysed, and I had to hold his papers so that he could tear them, I found out how absolutely *precisely* he worked. There was enormous control, and every tiny little bit of paper was torn and nitched to *exactly* the shape he wanted. This spiky bit here at the top, that little bit down there which is not quite rounded, this piece of blue which shows underneath in a sort of a circle, where he has torn a piece off; each of these things is meant to be like that. His control was much tighter than I could possibly have imagined.

These pieces work in a total way, with shape and colour and depth all giving an experience that is simultaneous, because of the structure underneath. It is very tight, yet they look quite loose and free. Francis used only used papers, so his colours are entirely *found*. But they are all put together so that they have a tonal relation, and a spatial relation; and the colour relation comes right when you get the tone and the structure right. "Right" means that every single bit of the picture works in about six different ways: you have all these things going on at once and they all relate to each other: backwards and forwards, flat surface against depth, colour through form.

Structure and colour

When something has gone wrong with a painting or *collage*, you tend to think it is the colour that is wrong, but it almost always turns out to be the shape or structure. Colour only works in amounts; it depends on *how much* blue, *how much* red, and how it's touching the other colours. To get colour to work you have to concentrate on the forms and the structure.

It is like music. People don't expect music to be a copy of something, do they? They realise it's a relationship of sounds to each other. What makes the music is the structure of the sounds, and it is exactly the same with painting and *collage*. The difference is that music is one sound *after* the other, whereas with a picture you are getting it all at once, there isn't any sort of progression. Your eye may move from one thing to another, but you are aware of the total area, and you don't have to look in any particular direction, it's not structured in time. I don't know why people have to expect paintings to represent something; they don't expect music to, they listen to the whole thing. And you ought to look at a painting or a *collage* in the way that you listen to music.

Southwold   September 1988

Jennifer Durrant

Influences

There was a space of a few years when a great deal that was important happened to me. It was the period after about '71 when I had begun to work in the studio at Stockwell Depot. I had been looking at Chinese scroll paintings and oriental artifacts and the glazing of porcelain in the British Museum. The paintings were painted on silk which had been already stained with colour, so the surfaces were not white, they were already beautiful colours, there was no perspective; and there was the combination of intricate detail and very large expanses of fluid description, of flowing garments, for example. And around the same time I had gone to the States for the first time, and seen contemporary American painting, and I realised that they had got colour into the surface in a different way from the way one had always known, which was by working on to a very well prepared surface, with paint which could be rubbed off. The idea of colour actually saturating and impregnating the surface, and making a visual statement from the start that had a very distinctive quality, was something very fresh and new to me.

I can see with hindsight that suddenly many considerations came together. I was learning a lot in an almost roundabout way. So although at art school you are encouraged to look at certain things and appreciate the masters, you come to things when you are ready. This is how it is now and I find it immensely exciting when I find something new for myself.

Painting, abstraction and reality

The first time I felt I identified with abstract painting was at the Richard Smith exhibition at the Whitechapel Gallery in 1964. Those were the first pictures about which I actually thought: well, now I understand; if this is what is abstract, then this makes sense to me. Their images were derived from, in the main, cigarette boxes, Marlborough packs, and primarily they were openly and broadly painted, with large areas of colour, not hard-edged at all. They were very striking, and, as mentioned in the catalogue, concerning densities of colour, (like the density of a hedge). That immediately rang bells with me. At that time I was painting some pictures about looking into a hedge with rose-bushes the other side; and I was at some sort of middle ground between on the one hand attempting to describe what I was seeing, and on the other, wanting to *express the experience* of being in a dense mass of a certain colour, with this vibrant, striking image within.

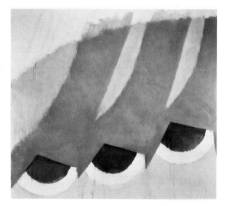

Richard Smith *Trio* 1963
Arts Council Collection

My paintings are not the conscious recreation of an exterior space; they are, perhaps, concerning my internal space. My thoughts and imaginings are prompted by those particular and quite distinct things that I observe in the outside world, and by my identification with them, and my feelings toward what I see.

I should mention the American painter Arthur Dove whose thoughts on painting I identify with strongly. He's not so well known here, but I would consider he was behind the modern American movement that I was influenced by in the early 70's. He had certain ideas about colour and about abstraction, although he didn't use the word abstract, he talked about *extraction*. He spoke about how he used his response to the outside world.

A Goodbye (to C and B) 1987

There and Back 1987

*Painting,
imagination and
contemplation*

A painting is not a description of the world; it is itself, it has to be. I am very questioning about what I consider illustrative or descriptive work, because although I think that in any good painting of whatever kind, one may sense a semblance of the outside world, there will always be a sense of mystery that takes it beyond imitation.

I believe I have a catholic taste in art, I enjoy many different sorts of painting, and if one does that, then one is faced with coming to terms with what is there in each of them, and in so doing, using differing parts of oneself in response to them.

I'm thinking of work by other artists: what they are making is their world, and if it is good, and it comes over strongly, and has all the natural qualities a fine painting has, then it takes you beyond, it takes you somewhere else. That is an important point for me; that I believe paintings are a vehicle. They are themselves, they have their own completeness, but that completeness is not only about staying there in front of the painting: I really do think that a painting is actually taking you off to some place else, of your own imagining.

I do think that a painting may be rather like a *mandala*, in the sense that its use may be of a meditative or contemplative sort. Contemplative is nearer to it: and that makes me think of certain works that are terribly important to me. One of those which has stayed with me for many years is the Giovanni Bellini – *Saint Francis in the Desert*; its contemplative qualities, its intricacies, its wonderful light, its sheer beauty, it transports you; it's simply wonderful. I feel the same way about paintings by Chardin, in which there is activity and yet a quiet stillness. I'm not thinking so much of the still-lifes, I'm thinking of those pictures with figures. There's one with the little boy playing with cards at a card-table: you're looking at a painting which is incredibly *constructed* in terms of formal devices, the angles of table and cards forcing you in and around the painting. The space is very mysterious in that you do not have a described background; it is like a blank wall. And there is the little boy totally engrossed in his activity with the cards; something is going on but it's very quiet; and yet the painting gives you a very powerful experience. That's something I identify with; I would like to think that something of that quality might at some point come through what I do; that is what I would aspire to.

That sort of achievement is mysterious. One doesn't set out to paint beautiful pictures, or to create mystery of that kind. I believe those things happen as a result of being in tune with both the practice of art and one's own inner awareness, and that when things are going well, and when one is in tune, then there is an inevitability that this will become apparent in whatever it is one is creating. You have to take that on trust. The intensity of your effort is repaid. You can always sense it in other people's work: you gravitate towards something that has that intensity.

Giovanni Bellini *St Francis in the Desert*
Frick Collection, New York

Jean Siméon Chardin *A House of Cards* c.1740
National Gallery, London

*Art and the
external
world*

Perhaps my favourite time of the day is when the light is beginning to go – fade, and there is an extraordinary quality of *thickness* in the air, a certain pitch of colour and of mood – a very particular sensation. It might prompt me to use a certain density of colour, a saturation of colour that I would then introduce elements into, aware that I am setting up something like an illusion of a three-dimensional world for myself, which to some extent is what I was doing. I already have a world that I could then inhabit.

The sort of experience I am talking about is very ordinary I presume. I am aware when I am taking the dog for a walk, or when I am in the country, that I am using what I see in a very conscious way, and bringing it back to the studio, (in thoughts or note-form). I can think of the example of coming across a tree where the prevailing wind and the rain had affected one side of the trunk, so that that side had a particular lime-green colour, and the other was a silvery purple, and I thought – that's interesting, that they are virtually complementaries, and I wrote a note on that, and I thought – how might I incorporate that in a painting? Thoughts about layers of glaze for example. I don't mean in an arbitrary way, I mean how it might fit with other things. I make a lot of notes, and obviously I use such considerations within a painting *if it seems appropriate to whatever else is going on.* But *not* to represent, not to describe what I have seen. It seems inevitable that a work is an amalgam of certain experiences. But the painting will create its own particular experience both because it is a painting made as it has been made, with all that that entails, and it is in some way a *distillation* of various experiences, and it must create of those things something new.

I make my large paintings on the floor because I want to work on a hard surface, (I can sandpaper the painting if necessary) and this involves me kneeling on the painting. I spend a lot of time moving up from the floor, where I am actually in the painting, and I can only see parts of it, to my steps, from where I can see the whole painting in my field of vision. My large paintings begin with me having only pencil notes/diagrams. I don't make preparatory notes in colour, (my smaller works on paper are often paintings in their own right), written notes about things I have seen, certain colours I have seen, or relationships I want to put together in a painting. I might stain the canvas all over, or in part, and I might then tear paper shapes and cover parts of the canvas with shapes, or cover the canvas with paper and cut out stencils with a stanley-knife, and then re-stain exposed parts of the canvas, and so on. This early process-procedure is very deliberate and considered, but I can't know what the visual effect is going to be. I know the initial colours I want to use, I know the procedures, but once it is set up, it begins to have its own life.

Making the paintings

I began working on a large scale at Stockwell in the early '70s. I had been to America, and that was my first experience of really seeing large scale contemporary work, and I had responded very positively and identified with it. I was working on very big canvases – 16 to 17 feet long – I had a big enough studio floor; and every day on my way to the studio I walked past a number of huge hoardings. I made some sort of correlation between the way I worked across the canvas, and how much you take in when you are actually moving past a surface, as opposed to when you stop and face it head on. There is a field which might stretch beyond the periphery of your vision, and at the same time something existing very much within the physical boundary of the rectangle, and, which though fixed might suggest a space beyond the confines of the stretcher.

All these things are still constants in painting, and I would say they are relevant to the way I work now.

Peckham   November 1988

25

JAMES HUGONIN

**Making
the
work**

I'd like to say something about how these paintings are made. They contain very many minute articulations of colour, which are developed over a long period of time, but they are all working towards a stillness, a stillness that contains within it innumerable minute changes. There is a paradox here: in order to get that point of stillness, it demands all the activity. It is always the goal in my painting that they should work towards a balanced equilibrium. In working I find that I am always acutely aware of things being balanced, not in an easy or obvious way, not in the way, say, that the top balances the bottom, but in a *tenuous way*, like something that is lightly held, or poised. Getting the painting to work that way necessitates many, many repeated patterns of marks, small units of colour building up to a finite structure. The paintings are made in rhythms of colour according to what I can only describe as an *intuitive logic*.

I always work close up to the painting; when I am working I stand very close, so all the decisions are actually made very near to the painting, and I can't really tell how the whole thing is going to resolve itself until it is finished and I can stand away from it. The element of time, over three or four months on a painting, and that element of detachment which comes from going over the surface maybe hundreds of times to actually make one painting, amount to a discipline that is analogous to meditation. I've got to feel totally in tune with the painting, and to feel at one with myself. Something that Edda Renouf, the American painter said about her work is, I think, very applicable to my own: "I do not live fast. My art is not fast, but in the rhythm of a calm heart beat.... Not production, but growth. Not a profession, but an experience in seeing, breathing, walking, hearing, feeling; then there is change." What this is saying is that the way I build these patterns of colour across the surface of the painting is inextricably linked to my whole being, to the way that I breathe, to the way that *I am.*

When I am working it is important that I don't focus on any one part of the painting in isolation. I work the whole painting with each pattern of colour, and then I will work with another, and then another, so the complexity of the surface is actually built up colour by colour. I never want the rhythms of a painting to repeat in obvious patterns; there is no regular system to the distribution of the marks. You will see that I am always working with curves or arcs of colour but they don't conform to any logical patterning over the whole surface. They are to do with a process of *accommodating*, by which I mean that when I put one rhythm down, one pattern of curves of colour, it will be counteracted by the next, by its complementary colour perhaps. It's like a process of patiently layering the surface so that in the end you get it to *flicker.*

Structure

If a painting really works, I think it gives a sort of richness of modulation, something you might get from listening to music. What pleasure do you get out of listening to a work of Bach, for instance? All it is, when you actually analyse it, is a series of repeated notes; but the pleasure you get from those repetitions, (and also, I would say, from colour modulated in a particular way), is enormous. I know that the pleasure derives from definite structures, patternings, repetitions, organisations of the sounds that follow certain structures, but I am thinking also that all really good music offers space to the listener to actually create his or her own sounds and patterns. Why Bach's music continues to absorb me is to do with more than structure alone: it is the fact that it

Extract from Briggflatts III 1987-88

Extract from Briggflatts IV 1987-88

alludes to something much freer. It is the structure which creates the space that allows the listener to "lose" himself in the music. This, I believe, is equally applicable to painting.

The grid I use is a forming principle, a structure to work with and to work against. It is a systematic structure imposed upon the surface, but if I use it inventively, it gives me tremendous freedom to create complexities of rhythm and pattern. I need something stable: the very regularity of the grid is needed to oppose the irregularities of the rhythms. All of these configurations that I put down are intuitively arrived at, they do not conform to any pre-planned system. I always want to make something which will defy the system I have initially imposed – the system of the grid itself.

It's important, again, to stress that I am very conscious of not creating specific or recognisable forms. All of the small marks with which I build up the painting must simply hold the picture plane; I don't want the marks to suggest obvious shapes or patterns. What I am working towards is an over-all shimmer on the surface; I want the painting to attain a quality as of shifting light.

Light and colour

In many ways I share an affinity with other painters like Monet and Rothko, when I say that I want the shimmer to be there. I mean it to work in that almost indescribable way, when you cannot be quite sure what the colour is that you perceive, that point where colour is indeterminate, somewhere between tone and pure colour. It could be said that the subject of these paintings is the fickleness and instability of light, and also of colour. With colour you are working with a very changeable substance: simply to put one colour next to another is to immediately change whatever relationships preceded that. There's a complexity and a simplicity here, an inextricable linking of colour and light.

I want my paintings to allude to this fleeting light in things; I want to put colours together in such a way that the juxtaposition turns back upon itself to give you another colour, almost a sensed colour. The colours in the paintings are in fact pure colours, clear blues and greens and so on; however, you can only see this when you are very close. It is only when you move back that these colours dissolve into something that is hardly a colour at all. Cézanne and Seurat were greatly interested in this. When you look closely at a Seurat painting you find it is actually built up of quite distinct complementary colours, but the merging of those complementaries at a distance creates a kind of scintillating greyness.

Georges Pierre Seurat *The Entrance to the Harbour at Gravelines* Courtauld Institute, London

Painting and reality

It is in the nature of my paintings that you can never look at them and see the same thing twice. They have no single focal point; there is no passage that is dominant. The eye may settle for a moment on a certain movement, but as it moves again across the painting that separated configuration will disappear into the matrix of marks and rhythms. Things continually disappear and re-form: things do not stay the same. This is absolutely crucial to my work: what I am trying to do is to present the evanescence of things, to heighten the fact that everything is in essence transitory.

Of course there is reference in my painting to the world outside: the "shimmer" I have spoken about is a quality of the light that plays on things in the natural world. I live in a beautiful place, in a place that has given me a great deal as a person. I feel that the place nurtures me. I love the quality of light up here in Northumberland, the way that light shifts across a surface. The way it picks out and suddenly accentuates certain aspects of the landscape, the fleeting light across a hillside: this quality of modulation in the real world that I see around me is a constant source of fascination. More than that, I feel that it has shaped my sensibility, and I want some of that feeling in the painting.

It is like that quality in the poetry of Basil Bunting, of the sound behind the words; there is something liberating about being able to concentrate on the musical rhythms and interweaving patterning of the words themselves. The poetry begins with the perceptions of real things, of natural phenomena, and so do the prints I made for Basil's poems, and so do my paintings, in a sense. But I feel that I have to deal with those things in the natural world at one step removed: it is important to me that the images I make are abstract images and not of reality as such. They are informed by the Northumberland landscape and the quality of its light, but the images I create are quite deliberately *another way of presenting that reality*.

Painting and the spectator

I think that my paintings require time. The inherent sensations in the painting, these very minute changes that I have been working with, actually work on the eye very slowly. These are very slow paintings, and I see the viewer's encounter with them very much as a continuous dynamic process. They are objects for contemplation. The paintings are in a sense only the starting point for a re-forming of the composition on the part of the viewer. The paintings demand a certain quality of individual involvement. It is in this sense that they confront a more hedonistic sensibility that wants everything at once, all in one go. I think you really have to look at the paintings with some degree of concentration for them to be enjoyed and absorbed.

Wooler Northumberland   September 1988

ALBERT IRVIN

Paintings and the world

These pictures are not in any sense *depictions* of anything: I like to think that rather than being pictures *of* the world, they are pictures *about* it, about experiencing proximity and distance, and aboveness and belowness, and over-thereness: they are about all these things we sense as we perambulate through the world, ride on tops of buses, walk the streets, travel on the underground. I got a great deal from the few conversations I had with Peter Lanyon: he used to do gliding and underwater swimming, and explore tin mines, as well as walking the Cornish cliffs and beaches, and he talked about *experiencing* the landscape – being above it, on it, below it. I feel there is a parallel between his landscape experience and my urban equivalent.

I do think that my paintings rely on my perceptions of the world at large, outside art, on my being in the world, moving through the world. There is never any reference to anything in particular, but there is no question about the fact that one has looked at a lot of paintings by other artists, and loved them all one's life, and there must be all sorts of things in the ragbag of visual ideas that one carries around, and these things must emerge in some way.

I didn't start out by thinking of this, but on reflection I realise that the rectangle of the canvas itself is two severe verticals and two severe horizontals, and that is the world I am inhabiting imaginatively when I am painting. And that is a metaphor for the urban world in which I live, which is bound by the verticals and horizontals of walls and floors and ceilings – the streets and rooms that are the containers I live in.

The way I title my paintings has to do with this directly. They are all given street names, which is a kind of symbol for what I was talking about. The paintings have to be identified, nothing more, just as streets have to be identified. I started with the streets around my studio, but I've painted so many pictures that eventually I ran out of names. But by then I had convinced myself of the validity of the procedure, and I felt that wherever I was, or if circumstances suggested it for some other reason, then I could use any street name that I came across that had some sort of association or relevance for me. The paintings *Broadway* and *Madison* in the present show were made just after a marvellous trip to New York. *Easter* is named after Easter Road in Edinburgh, which is a place I visit a lot. I thought of various names, but this one seemed to be dragging "Easter" towards itself. Of course presenting that title to a painting that has a great burst of yellow light, and has a structure based on three near verticals, is bound to bring out a lot of other associations. But I would want to say this about any painting: it is something that exists for the spectator to discharge his own imagination into. All a painter can say is – I've given you this, and I've written the title underneath, and what you do with it now I really have no control over, *nor do I want to have.*

Space and Scale

A painting can have scale even if it is small. (A page in a Constable sketchbook, for example, has real scale, imaginative scale.) But one of the things that I would like to feel I can explore and exploit in a large canvas is just the fact that the top of it is above you, the bottom of it below you, the left of it away to the spectator's left and the right sweeping away to the right; so that not only has it got this *imaginative scale*, that something in a sketchbook might have, it has also got this direct *perceptual* scale. Think of the way that James Ward painted *Gordale Scar*: he wanted the size and scale of the

Easter 1984

Broadway 1988

canvas itself to be a kind of metaphor for the vertiginousness and monumentality of it, the sheer *overhangingness* of the thing that he was painting. It is that sort of thing that I feel is possible on a large canvas, that you can't get on a small one.

I wouldn't want to describe it as an "environment", but on the other hand, it can't be ignored that it is that, in the sense that it might impress you in the same way as a landscape, or a sky, or an expanse of water does, just by virtue of its size. I like to try to use these aspects of scale as elements in the painting that I am doing, which is, nevertheless, a thing in its own right.

Colour plays a great part in it; colour is one of the elements there. But I think the prime element of painting is space. You know, it is in space where it all happens; as the prime element in music is time, in which the whole thing unfolds. All these factors that we employ – colour and line and tone and form and so on – are all part of the fabric of space.

One of the intriguing things for me about painting, one of the reasons why I am a painter rather than a sculptor, is that it is an illusion one is playing with. The canvas is a flat thing; there isn't any real three-dimensional space in a picture, actual space, there is only virtual space. You can run your hand over the canvas and confirm that the thing is flat. The difference between the space of a sculpture and the space of a painting is that a sculpture is like that table – if you want to find out what is happening on the other side, you walk round it to the other side, whereas with a painting the only way you can experience any depth that the artist has wanted to include in it is by imaginative projection into it.

In my earlier paintings the shapes and forms tended to butt up against each other and squeeze out any space between them; they spread across the canvas, the surface was intact, you couldn't get in anywhere. Then I wanted to put things in front of one another, for my paintings to relate to perceptual reality as we experience it in the real space of the world.

Colour   Colour is for me, clearly, a big factor, and it has become increasingly important over the years. Earlier, my colours were not so high key as they have become, but I can identify a growing ambition to take on the problem of trying to make a painting with gravity and presence and yet employ high key colours. There is a great danger in this: you might finish up with the thing looking garish, like a disco, but if you're not courting danger I don't think you are taking on the problem. I mean, obviously, artists like Matisse have had a terrific influence in this respect. Matisse could put a red and a blue and a yellow and a green and black and white together and achieve a perfect clarity, a painting of great weight and dignity. Here is a beautiful statement from Matisse about this: "When the means of expression have become so refined and attenuated that the expressive power wears thin, it is time to return to the essential principles . . . pictures which have become refinements, subtle gradations, transmissions without force, call for beautiful blues, reds, yellows, matter to stir the sensual depths in men. That is the starting point of *Fauvism*, the courage to return to the purity of means."

The making of the paintings

One of the things that I would want to emphasise is how the paint is actually handled. I couldn't think of making a painting where the actual inflections in the paint, the trail of the artist, the passage of the individual who made the marks across the canvas, were not apparent. In a sense the painting is like a visible diary of events: at a certain moment in real time I left my mark there, and a record of the speed or slowness, the inflection or the expansiveness, of that gesture of red, that gesture of green, that gesture of blue. This aspect of the work is bound to act as a sort of contradiction to the elements of space, of recession and illusion, and it is these contradictions which make the painted surface intriguing. (de Kooning called it "no-space": he meant you spend all this time trying to make things look as if they are in front of each other, when you can see that it's just a load of paint jammed up against the canvas.) Matisse once said something like, "the trouble is the young people will think its easy!" I try to make my paintings look as if they just happened like that, but in fact they are absolutely, precisely constructed. Each colour has its place located quite definitely, the proportions and weight, the choice and the areas of colour are all worked out during the painting. These paintings haven't arrived by chance or gesture, or by accident: as Pollock said, *there are no accidents*. If you set the process up, you manoeuvre the process into accepting whatever happens; each move follows the last move, and so on: you discover it, you find it in the process. When you find the right colour or shape, you're on it like a hawk!

Why I paint

To come back to the question of abstract painting, I do think that it has set up a challenge during my time, which I have accepted. Turner was getting close to losing the image entirely, you know, in the late great paintings – like *Norham Castle* for example – but he was still looking at something, and painting it. But the problem above all others, for better or worse, that has been offered to my generation to deal with is this: can we paint all these great things about life and the world and so on, and still not have to depict? Can I make a painting about a human being, about the human spirit, without having to paint noses and feet? In a sense what I am saying is that these pictures are expressions of feeling, but also constructions that I make, using these particular elements, in order to create a particular effect upon the viewer that is life-affirming. I do believe in what Schopenhauer said: that all art seeks an answer to the question, *what is life?* I am very aware that life is a being until death. I am very aware; I mean, I got my bus-pass last year; I haven't far to go. I am very aware that when I am working on a canvas I am a living, pulsating, loving being. It is that that makes the work, and if only I can get that awareness into the paintings, then I believe they must speak to other human beings about those things that are happening to them, and to me. That is the ambition; and I would be mad if I didn't attempt it.

Stepney Green   September 1988

EDWINA LEAPMAN

Paintings and reality

I have always had a great reluctance to speak about my work: the paintings were things that I, as an artist, could hide behind. I feel that any explanation I might seem to give would mis-direct the viewer. And when I do speak, I often feel my words have changed what the painting might do or be about. Perhaps I feel that I limit, with my words, the real thing that the painting might communicate. We know now, from modern science and philosophy, and from psychology, that the observer alters what is observed, just by being present. Really it is the viewer's participation that gives the work its real life, that brings out its meaning.

My paintings are not about anything seen; they are only about themselves, and they exist in order to be seen. They don't depict external objects in any way; and neither do they express any mood, or emotion. And my works are not in any sense narrative, but they do carry a history. Not in a personal sense, or in the sense of the history of their own making, but rather in relation to my experience of the history of art; they couldn't have been made without that knowledge.

Why I like looking at certain paintings – at Piero della Francesca for example, or at Paul Klee, to take two artists a long way apart – is that they bring me back to my own centre, my truth, my own being; and that having been given that sense of being, having been put back firmly into myself, I can look out from within and say that was *that* person's being. It is like remembering something you have forgotten, something you really do know, but which you keep forgetting. I don't want my paintings to say it all at once, at full blast so to speak, as some paintings do, and make you reel from the shock of it, be bowled over in one go. I don't want my works to be drama, they are not theatre.

I would like to think that my paintings were restorative, like going to a quiet place, breathing fresh air. I hesitate to commit myself to a word like 'spiritual' – it is so misused, it has so many connotations – but my work reflects my interest, over many years, in the writings of the great mystics; and it has to do with those things that are the concern of philosophy and psychology, things which have always interested me.

When I was at the Slade in the late fifties I painted in a figurative style, and most of my friends at that time were music students. I used to make drawings of them playing, string quartets, trios. I developed these into paintings, but I was always dissatisfied; and then I realised that what I was really trying to do was not to paint the musicians, *but to paint the music.* I had only been illustrating the idea, when what I really wanted to do – and I still want to do this – was to make the thing itself, with no obvious link with the external objects, the bodies, the instruments etc. I am still trying to develop a true and direct expression of that "thing itself"; in fact really I think in some ways I still want to paint music.

Colour and light

Colour cannot exist without tone: that was perhaps my first understanding of painting, and it's probably the basis of what I do today. Tone can mean pitch– that is, where and how to place colour in a painting on a scale, as in music: up towards the top, high keyed, bright; or slow in the bass registers, where it is difficult to distinguish all the sounds. Colour and tone to me mean light, light in all its manifestations: the light of dawn moving towards the light of the day; the different light of dusk, more mysterious, moving towards the darkness of night. I want the paintings to have a luminosity, or

Enharmonic dark blue and red 1988

Enharmonic blue 1988

more precisely, a dark light: I know that's a paradox, but the darker a painting, the more it seems to me to emanate light. It's like the intense darkness of an after-image.

There is a piece by Beckett that also seems to describe my attempts (attempts at the impossible perhaps!): "...staring out at nothing just failing light quite still till dark though of course no such thing just less light still when less did not seem possible."*

Space

And light in its turn means space: in my paintings a pictorial space, hovering (I like to think) both in front of the surface as well as on the surface, and below the surface. To these qualities of colour and tone, and light, I must add air: I like to think that my paintings provide a space where people can breathe. To breathe is to live; breath is the spirit that animates the body: the colour, light and space in my paintings combine in a sort of pulsating, expanding and contracting sensation like breathing – but apprehended visually.

A lot of paintings don't give you space, don't allow you to breathe; they're claustrophobic. Sometimes, on Hampstead Heath, in the stillness before a storm, the space seems almost tangible and measured, and the air is so heavy it seems possible to grasp it with your hands, and the trees recede into the distance in measured layers. Something of that tangibility of space is partly what my paintings are about.

Scale and physicality

I think that the physicality of paintings is paramount. I like to work on paintings that are too big for me, uncomfortable to encompass physically, so that my hand, awkward and shaky as it is, has to move along as I move from side to side – I actually walk that move, and then from top to bottom of the canvas – I have to use steps. And the paint is physical stuff, there's no getting away from that, it's pigment, earth, ground rock. Working at a physical scale bigger than is really comfortable might stretch and extend me beyond my own limitations, it might take me that much further than I anticipate at the beginning.

Structure

I'm always being asked about the parallel lines that are the underlying structure of the work. Its often implied that they represent a sort of limitation – "why don't you become freer?" sort of thing. Well, actually, lines have a great deal of meaning for me: I've used a linear structure for the last fifteen years or so. Ruled parallel lines, over which I paint from left to right, starting at the top left hand corner, and moving over, line by line, and down the canvas. It's just like reading a book, as you read and scan the lines, and that's one way of looking at the paintings. What lines really mean for me is complete freedom; I know people will say, that doesn't look free, it looks very organised, but it is actually free, because once they are there I can forget them. It's like sitting on a chair with a back to it, you don't have to try not to fall backwards. It's not a limitation; it just means I can do what I want without falling off my chair, so to speak.

Of course, its a formal device, and it enables me to get on with the application of paint in a way that has directness of touch. The straight bands are a guide, they are a means, they are the width of a brush more or less. Having pencilled the lines across the

* Samuel Beckett "Still" (collected in *For To End Yet Again* John Calder, London 1976)

canvas, I then build up layers and layers of colours in thin transparent washes, which are there to negate each other. So if I have a red, I will probably put a green on it, and then another red on top of that, and then perhaps a blue, until I have a ground which is dense and intense, but indeterminate in colour. You can't be quite sure what it is, it depends on the light, and your familiarity; that appeals to my imagination, and I hope to the viewer's. The paintings need to be watched, given time, be seen in changing conditions of light, allowed to become what they are.

There's always a contingent element: a not-knowing of what it is going to be like. You can never think a painting, you can only do it. It really doesn't come from the head. I would hate to make a painting already formed in my mind, and in a sense just reproduce that image on to canvas. The work is a discovery of something that finally feels authentic. And there must be absolutely no fiddling. Because then you begin to construct the painting in a known way. I want to construct a painting in an *unknown* way, unknown to me. I don't want to *design* a painting.

Belsize Park   October 1988

KENNETH MARTIN

Abstraction, and reality

Abstract art is truly objective not "non-objective". The object which is created is real and not illusional in that it sets out to represent no object outside the canvas, but to contain within itself the force of its own nature. And the painter seeks to be wholly intelligible in thus objectifying his subjective self. He attempts to create a universal language as against a private language.[1]

Signs and symbols have an organic-kinetic origin. Born of events and growing through their cumulation they decline in power through saturation or neglect and are born again from the primitive source or gain fresh life through transplantation or fusion. Abstract painting, where there is an insistence on the absolute reality of the marks made and of their interrelation, has shown fresh mastery of the power of the right angle, the diagonal, simple or complex rhythms and so forth, that is, *of the primitive sources of the symbol.*[2]

The horizontal, the vertical, slopes and curves, spaces, rhythm, colours can have a power over us. Why? Because of their effect on our spiritual, physical and mental make up. Because of their relationship with these, their accord and discord. Actually they are the world within and the world without, there to affect us at all times. They are universals and can be used to build up a structure to express and affect ourselves and also, modified by circumstance and personality, to do this for others in a similar way.[3]

There are three realities to be considered. The reality outside the artist, the reality inside him and the reality of the work he is making. These are universal no matter what kind of art is being made. The reality of the world outside, of course, includes everything. For the artist there is his own structure and metabolism and also his sense of reality. With regard to the work, each mark or line etc. which is being made has its own inherent realness and it is that the abstract constructivist artist uses. Between the three realities are correspondences which can be simplified to states of being that are acted upon by forces of change or are subject to conditions of change. The three realities are three metabolisms.[4]

Space and time

All streets, gardens, buildings, entrances, rooms, etcetera can produce different feelings in us as we move through them. The succession of these feelings can be organised to produce a totality of experience so that architecture can give us an ordered delight through its use of space, form and colour, as we rest and as we move, as we go about our everyday experience.[5]

My concern is my day. In 1967 my wife Mary wrote "We are always the same person but the situations in which we are placed are never identical, though they may be similar. At another time the repetition of situations may become so monotonous to us that we are compelled to change our position in order to maintain our sanity, or growth. All men may be the same everywhere but each one is different, and no two places are the same. We say 'Good Morning' every morning, but it is never the same morning; we are all a day older and our feelings vary. The artist, a part of nature, seeks to discover and use forming principles in order that he may in his turn manifest nature."[6]

Chance Order Change 13 'Milton Park A' (blue red green) 1980

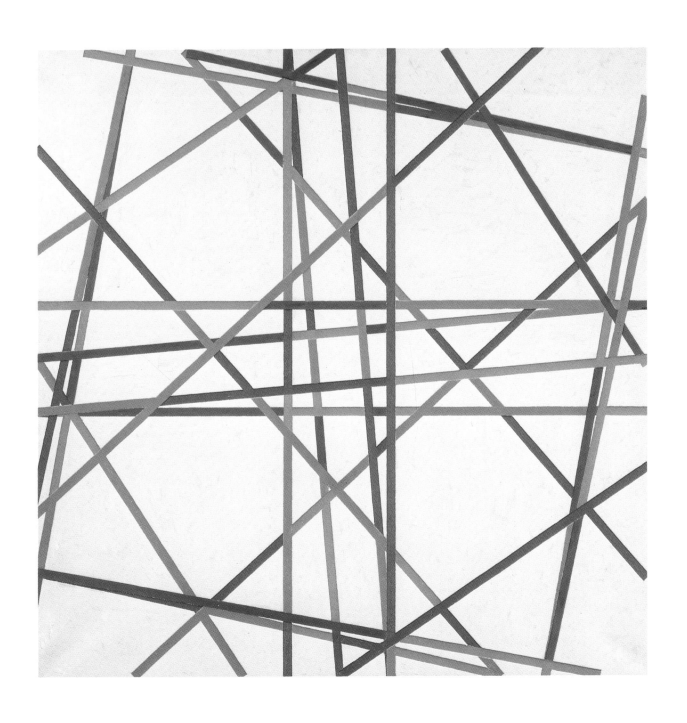

Chance Order Change 18 (4 colours) 1981

Art and the
external
world

A mark is made. What kind of force has it as it now exists? What power has it to be changed and what power can change it? What relationship can it play with other associated marks? What kind of interaction can take place?

Objects have an inherent power over us apart from all sentiment. (The still life painting is a manifestation of this.) The abstract, constructed work uses this power.

Awareness of sensation can vary from the acute to the subliminal and have an effect upon the spirit. Environmental sensations (e.g. those of passing under or over). Sensations of light and darkness. Those caused by colour. Those caused by direction and change of direction. These are both means and content.[7]

When I was told "you cannot do without nature" it was meant that I could not do without the speaker's view of nature, which was the sum of many self-selected views of nature. Nature changes because our conception of it and our physical attitude within it changes. (Art changes because our concern with life changes. It is that – a changing concept of life – which brings about and carries forward new art movements of any powerfulness.)[8]

Art corresponds with man's attitude to nature and with the feelings of life within himself.[9]

Structure

A drawn straight line has length, size and scale
> a beginning and an end.˙
> a direction
> a thickness
> a texture and a colour
> two sides when drawn on the plane
> a position in space
> it is a division of space
> space – line – space

The abstract constructed work is autonomous, but its laws are natural laws. It has great limitations. By using the properties of its elements, their position in space relative to one another, and truly constructing the work, there is a possibility of a variety of expressive forms. I am interested in the difference of the one straight line from the two, three or four or more parallel lines. There is a very great change of character – a leap – from the first to the second, a path has been created. And then the parallels can go on to being lines of companies, battalions, regiments, armies until anonymity brings complete unity within diversity – a field.[10]

The artist constructs with forces and the results of forces. He, himself, is a bundle of forces as in his work.

The work of art holds opposites within itself, horizontal against vertical, acute angle against straight, open against closed and so on.[11]

My work is kinetic whether the result is still or moving, therefore I am concerned with change – and with chance.... [12]

In 1969 I realised I could develop drawings by the use of chance. I could make a sequence independent of my personality. I could be the spectator. Hence "chance and order". These works were not made by knowledge and erudition. All was discarded except a numbered field, the character of the activity of the drawing of lines and my sense of art with which to start at the beginning again. [13]

And it was chance that helped me to go further with a painting because before I had always started with a doodle.... Now I can get the *dramatis personae* from number, I can start from the very beginning with number, the number gives a rhythm and points in space. In that respect I am using number like the composers did, like Bach, you start with an abstract set of numbers which is what I do.... You can develop order but not chance, you can only use chance again. This use of chance is the big thing for me and then this use of order. [14]

It is necessary to be forever beginning at the beginning. [15]

(Note: sources for the passages in this text will be found on p. 62)

Chance,
Order,
Change

BRIDGET RILEY

Colour,
form and
space

Braque spoke about the space of cubism, and Picasso always of the form; and although one defines the other, their approach is diametrically opposed. To speak about the space in a painting is less immediately clear than to speak of the form. Form implies shape, volume, parts which are nearer, parts which are farther, and that defines the space. If you start with space you have to put forms into it which articulate it coherently. It is a more difficult concept, but it is one to which Modern painting, with its emphasis on colour, subscribes. In Renaissance painting, broadly speaking, the forms describe positions in perspectival space, but when painters first tried to put colour on to those forms they found that an object in the background could appear to be on the same plane as one in the foreground. They discovered that colour took up positions of its own, independent of any linear or perspectival concept.

In the real world one identifies everything instantaneously; colours are seen in their different materials, as leaves, atmosphere, earth, water, skin, clothes of silk or satin, etc. But in *painting – it is one medium, one material, throughout*; it doesn't have this *actual* underpinning, the attachment of colour to real things. That's where the problem breaks open. Colour activity is incomparably stronger in painting than in external reality. This is something that all good painters know to different degrees; but imagine what it must have been like to wrestle with this in the teeth of a rigid pictorial organisation such as systematic perspective. It was the Impressionists who in their different ways took the form and space that colour makes as the determining factor in organising a painting.

Paul Cézanne *Le Château de Medan* c.1880
Burrell Collection, Glasgow City Art
Galleries

Whilst Modern painters have probably learnt most about the space that colour-forms make from Cézanne; there's been a tendency to think that Monet is merely beautiful. (As Cézanne said, "only an eye" – adding though, – "but what an eye!") His great weakness in many people's minds has been that his paintings are not structured. In fact, Monet's paintings *are* structured – and as radically so as Cézanne's – but *according to a different perceptual experience.* Monet paints what it seems to me we actually experience in looking, the drift and gather of sight itself. In those late water lily paintings he achieved a sort of perfection after a lifetime of research, *as a painter*, into the nature of perception itself.

Space
and
movement

There is seldom a single focal point in my paintings; generally, my paintings are multi-focal. You can't call it un-focussed space, but not holding on to a single focus is very much of our time; it's something that has come about in the last hundred years or so. Focussing isn't just a physical activity, it is also a mental one. I think this has to do in some way with the loss of the certainties that Christianity had to offer: there was a time when focus could enable meanings to be found, reality to be fixed; when that sort of focus disappeared, meanings became more difficult to fix. We can no longer believe as they did in the Renaissance that "man is the measure of all things".

We are not concerned with a search for a focus because it is generally felt, I think, that such a thing is no longer possible, and other ways of paying attention to things that matter have to be found. This is something that has happened in other arts as well. Proust, for example, is actually a writer without a single focal point, and so is much of Samuel Beckett; some modern music and, again, Monet's late water lily paintings. It is all to do with the loss of certainties. Nevertheless, in losing this focus we find ourselves

Isfahan 1984

Ease 1987

Claude Monet *Water Lilies* c.1916-23
National Gallery, London

exposed to enigmatic, unknown experiences, things that were previously less accessible.

In my earlier paintings I regarded the picture plane as a point of departure, I wanted the space between it and the spectator to be active. It was in that space that the painting took place. Then, little by little, to some extent deliberately, I made it go the other way, opening up the interior, so that there was a layered shallow depth. It is important that the painting can be *inhabited*, so that the mind's eye, or the eye's mind can move about in it credibly.

I discovered a well-known principle (it's always exciting when you find things for yourself): that you cannot have movement without its opposite – stasis. There is no change without a constant. If you can bring the two things together in an image you have a dynamic, something that is not descriptive of movement, but which gives the sensation of it. For instance, in the painting *Descending* every other vertical is straight, and evenly disposed across the canvas. So that the movement goes a zigzag progress through alternating straight and curving verticals, from a narrow closing at the top left descending to the narrow strip of diagonals at the bottom right. It is one thing against another. In the recent paintings it is the active diagonals that are countered by the static verticals. (Cézanne knew, from his love of the great Venetians, that the diagonal is an activating force in countering the slow backwards and forwards pulse of colour.)

Making the paintings

People sometimes ask me how the paintings were made, and I always find that an odd question. Everything about the painting is there to be seen on the actual surface opposite the spectator. The paintings themselves answer their question; there is nothing I can add to what I have put down there. I know that might sound as though I were evading the issue, but it is actually true.

In making the paintings I proceed step by step, and test the ground before I make a move. And it may be that which gives the impression that my approach is programmatic. Actually, it's a process of trial and error, around the finding of the next move. I dream about what I am going to do, or rather about the sensations I want the painting to precipitate or convey. It's actually bringing those effects about that is the difficulty, what Cézanne called *"realisation"*. Not only is it extremely elusive, but being perceptual it is as much in our own nature as it is 'out there' in the external world. I used to set out to capture it as if one were casting a net to catch sensation and make it visible. Now I build it up, make a sort of fabric with places in it so there is more variety of situation.

Copying is the old way of learning. In 1959 I made a copy of Seurat's *Le Pont de Courbevoie*. "Doing the same" is a way of getting closer than you ever can by simply observing. I learnt a great deal, and some of the implications of what I had experienced then only became clear to me much later. At that time I came across the wonderful review of Seurat's work by Félix Fénéon, in which he says: "…here in truth the accidents of the brush are futile, trickery is impossible; there is no place for bits of bravura, – let the hand be numb, but let the eye be agile, perspicacious, cunning."

Bridget Riley copy after Seurat *'Le pont de Courbevoie'* 1959 Private Collection

Painting and reality

When I made the first black and white painting, I did not intend to make more than one. And then I became interested; I thought perhaps I can try one more. The first one hadn't done quite what I wanted, which was to say something, as a very personal message to a particular person about the nature of things. At that point in time I wanted to say: that *there were absolutes*; that one could not pretend that black was white. I wanted to make a deliberate statement, to make a thing that put itself into hazard by some aspect of its own nature. And that was the beginning of the black and white paintings. People at the time thought (and some people still seem to think it) that they were paintings having to do with optical experiment (and "Op Art" and so on); really they were an attempt to say something about stabilities and instabilities, certainties and uncertainties. They were never simply about how fascinating it might be to take black and white and put them together into those optically dynamic configurations.

Colour and form

I also learnt a lot about colour from copying Seurat. His "method" as he called it, is more accessible than, say, the way Cézanne and Monet thought about colour. But I still did not realise for a very long time to what a profound extent the basis of colour is instability. An element so responsive to relationships and interaction as colour is cannot be absolute and stable in the way that forms described by line can be. A square is a square. It is an absolute. One knows when a form deviates from a square. It's conceptually fixed. But a blue…! The hues of blue are infinite, and the same blue will look different in different contexts: in reality, and more crucially, in a painting. One never sees a colour isolated, and so you never know exactly *what any particular colour is*. On a canvas, true, it is physical paint, but a colour is not material. Each shade gives off a different light, and these interact according to what is next to what, where they are in the whole, and what their *quantities* are.

In the Egyptian paintings of the early '80s, (that was a studio name for them; I made them after a visit to Egypt, and their colours were influenced by that experience) I chose long thin verticals, because the stripe has very little body, it's mostly edges. The interaction between colours is most dynamic when one colour borders on another; stripes maximise this relationship. They were made vertical so that the spectator would scan across horizontally and encounter the varying frictions set up.

It was in those paintings that I began to build with these sensations directly. In that review I quoted just now by Fénéon he says something else very much to the point: "These colours, isolated on the canvas, recombine on the retina: we have therefore, not a mixture of material colours (pigments) but a mixture of differently coloured rays of light." That is right – but it's not simply light waves in the scientific sense of wave lengths. It's more as though the colour is breathing, giving off a subtly tinted cloud of its own transformed energy. It happens all the time in nature, but it comes into its own in painting: it is the miracle of colour itself.

London   November 1988

Born in London, 1930. Studied at Camberwell School of Art. During the 1950s worked at the AIA Gallery in Lisle Street, London. Taught at Bath Academy of Art, Corsham, 1959-65, St Martin's School of Art, 1966-78 and, as Head of Painting, at Winchester School of Art, 1978-81. Began visiting Wales regularly in 1951, and lived and worked in North Wales, 1981-88. Now lives in Cornwall. Elected an ARA in 1982. Awarded OBE in 1986. Had major one person exhibitions at the Museum of Modern Art, Oxford in 1981, and the Serpentine Gallery, London and Mostyn Art Gallery, Llandudno in 1984. An exhibition of recent paintings is planned by the Arnolfini Gallery, Bristol in 1989. Exhibits regularly at the Knoedler Gallery, London.

Wells 1982
oil on canvas, 213.4 diameter
Courtesy Knoedler Kasmin Ltd

Where Phoebus first did Daphne love 1983
oil on canvas, 182.9 x 182.9 (hexagon)
Collection Sam Mundy

Tallis 1984
oil on canvas, 213.4 x 182.9
Courtesy Knoedler Kasmin Ltd

Fairest of Stars 1984
oil on canvas, 334.8 x 182.9
Courtesy Knoedler Kasmin Ltd

A Painted Tale 1985
oil on canvas, 243.8 x 274.8
Courtesy Knoedler Kasmin Ltd

Aquina 1986
oil on canvas, 243.8 diameter
Courtesy Knoedler Kasmin Ltd

Widecombe Fair 1987
oil on canvas, 262.9 x 201.9
Courtesy Knoedler Kasmin Ltd

Hydaspes 1988
oil on canvas, 244.2 x 157.5
Courtesy Knoedler Kasmin Ltd

Untitled 1988
oil on canvas, 91.4 x 61 (oval)
Collection J & S Mundy

Born in London, 1919; died in Southwold, 1984. Brought up by adoptive parents in France and England. Read English and Anthropology at Cambridge. Wrote poetry but began to draw in 1946. Married Margaret Mellis 1948. Early married months in France. Moved to Suffolk 1950, Walberswick, then Syleham where they kept a small-holding until 1976, and finally Southwold. By the early '50s his paintings became simplified to arrangements of flat shapes. Began making collages 1952. During the '60s and '70s he introduced a wider range of colours and dispensed with any reference to landscape. One person exhibitions at the Graves Art Gallery Sheffield 1981, Museum of Modern Art, Oxford 1982 and the Hayward Gallery, London 1983. Since his death the Redfern Gallery has mounted two exhibitions.

All works are coloured paper collages. Titles are not the artist's and have been applied posthumously. Dates are generally approximate.

Blue green red and fawn with navy edges
61.0 x 73.7
Private Collection

Pink green black brown
71.1 x 67.3
Private Collection

Garden collage 1981
86.0 x 88.8
Private Collection

Blue with white ochre and brown c.1984-6
110.5 x 122
Private Collection

Green black and brown c.1976-78
109.2 x 110.5
Private Collection

Yellow with square hole c.1978-82
95.3 x 125.1
Private Collection

Winds of colour
114 x 129
Private Collection

Red yellow green black purple with empty square 1978-83
115.6 x 147
Private Collection

White ground with pink brown and green 1984
146.1 x 146.1
Private Collection

Blue with white rectangle and square hole 1984
146.1 x 146.1
Private Collection

Flashing light and dark colours c.1978-83
176.5 x 139.7
Private Collection

Crossed paths 1978-81
176.5 x 146.1
Private Collection

Large green 1982
175.3 x 144.8
Private Collection

Born in Brighton, 1942. Studied at Brighton College of Art and Slade School of Fine Art. Has taught at various colleges; currently teaches at the Royal College of Art and Chelsea School of Art. One person exhibitions include the Arnolfini Gallery, Bristol 1979, Museum of Modern Art, Oxford 1980, Nicola Jacobs Gallery 1982 and 1985, Northern Centre for Contemporary Art, Sunderland 1986, and Serpentine Gallery, London 1987. Winner of the Athena Prize 1988. Lives and works in London.

Fading 1985-6
acrylic on canvas, 259.7 x 284
Collection, the Artist

Passing 1986
acrylic on canvas, 259.7 x 231.9
Collection, the Artist

Fallen (yellows) 1986
acrylic on canvas, 259.1 x 309.8
Collection, the Artist

After La Fenice 1986-7
acrylic on canvas, 259.7 x 309.8
Collection, the Artist

A Goodbye (to C. and B.) 1987
acrylic on canvas, 259.7 x 304.8
Collection, the Artist

Nearing the End No. 2 1987
acrylic on canvas, 259.7 x 310
Collection, the Artist

There and Back 1987
acrylic and some metallic paint on canvas, 216.6 x 335.2
Collection, the Artist

The One is the Other 1988
acrylic on canvas, 304.8 x 254
Collection, the Artist

JAMES HUGONIN

Born in Barnard Castle, Durham 1950. Studied at Winchester School of Art, West Surrey College of Art and Design, Chelsea School of Art. Has taught at Chelsea School of Art and colleges in the North East. One person exhibitions include Galerie Brigitte Hilger, Aachen 1983, Coracle, London 1985, Graeme Murray Gallery, Edinburgh 1985 and Bede Gallery, Jarrow 1985, Cairn Gallery, Nailsworth, Gloucestershire 1986 and Galerie Hoffman, Friedberg 1987. Lives and works in the Cheviots, Northumberland.

Untitled XV 1984-88
oil/wax on plywood, 152.4 x 137.2
Collection, the artist

Untitled XIV 1984-87
oil/wax on plywood, 152.4 x 137.2
Private Collection, Frankfurt

Painting for Basil Bunting 1985
oil/wax on plywood, 22.2 x 18.8
Private Collection, Frankfurt

Study for Untitled XVII part 2 1986
oil/wax on plywood, 25.4 x 22.8
Private Collection, London

Study for Untitled XVII part 4 1985
oil/wax on plywood, 22.2 x 18.8
Private Collection, Friedberg

Untitled XVII 1985
oil/wax on plywood, 152.4 x 137.2
Collection, the artist

October Painting 1986
oil/wax on plywood, 25.4 x 22.8
Private Collection, Wiesbaden

Untitled XVIII 1986
oil/wax on plywood, 152.4 x 137.2
Courtesy Galerie Hoffman, Friedberg

Untitled XIX 1988
oil/wax on plywood, 152.4 x 137.2
Collection, the artist

Untitled 1988-89
oil/wax on plywood, 170.2 x 152.4
Collection, the artist

Four paintings for
Extract from Briggflatts I-IV 1987-88
oil/wax on plywood, each 33 x 26
Collection, the artist

ALBERT IRVIN

Born in London 1922. Studied at Northampton School of Art, and Goldsmiths' School of Art. Taught at Goldsmiths' 1962-83. Recent one person exhibitions include Newcastle Polytechnic Gallery 1978, Bede Gallery, Jarrow 1980, Gimpel and Weitzenhoffer, New York, 1988. Represented by Gimpel Fils Gallery, London. Lives and works in London.

Renfrew 1983
acrylic on canvas, 244 x 427
Courtesy Gimpel Fils

Easter 1984
acrylic on canvas, 213 x 305
Private Collection

Madison 1988
acrylic on canvas, 213 x 305
Courtesy Gimpel Fils

Broadway 1988
acrylic on canvas, 213 x 305
Courtesy Gimpel Fils

Holyrood 1988
screen print, 137.8 x 105.7
Courtesy Gimpel Fils

Holyrood II 1988
screen print, 137.8 x 105.7
Courtesy Gimpel Fils

EDWINA LEAPMAN

Studied at Slade School of Fine Art and the Central School of Arts and Crafts. Lives and works in London. Exhibits at Annely Juda Fine Art.

Enharmonic deep blue 1988
acrylic on cotton, 193 x 165.1
Courtesy Annely Juda Fine Art

Enharmonic blue 1988
acrylic on cotton, 182.9 x 134.6
Courtesy Annely Juda Fine Art

Enharmonic indeterminate brown 1988
acrylic on linen, 165.1 x 182.9
Courtesy Annely Juda Fine Art

Enharmonic blue on pink 1988
acrylic on cotton 198.1 x 152.4
Courtesy Annely Juda Fine Art

Enharmonic tall maroon 1988
acrylic on cotton, 229.2 x 152.4
Courtesy Annely Juda Fine Art

Enharmonic turquoise red 1988
acrylic on cotton, 213.4 x 162.6
Courtesy Annely Juda Fine Art

Enharmonic dark blue and red 1988
acrylic on cotton, 198.1 x 152.4
Courtesy Annely Juda Fine Art

Enharmonic Series 1988

An enharmonic note is like a word with two spellings and one meaning. On the piano C sharp and D flat are represented by the same black key and they are described as enharmonically equivalent. The term derives from the ancient Greek theoretical system which admitted the existence of smaller intervals than the semitone.

E.L.

KENNETH MARTIN

Born in Sheffield 1905, died in London 1984. Studied at Sheffield School of Art and the Royal College of Art, London. Lived and worked in London. Visiting teacher at Goldsmiths' School of Art 1946-67. Began first abstract paintings 1948-49, first kinetic constructions 1951, first *Chance and Order* works 1969. Awarded OBE 1971. One person exhibitions include Tate Gallery, London 1975. Yale Center for British Art, New Haven, Connecticut 1979 and Serpentine Gallery, London 1985. Estate represented by Annely Juda Fine Art.

Chance Order Change 1 (15 colours) 1976
oil on canvas, 121.9 x 121.9
Private Collection

Chance Order Change 2 (ultramarine blue) 1976
oil on canvas, 91.4 x 91.4
Arts Council Collection

*Chance Order Change 13 'Milton Park A'
(blue red green)* 1980
oil on canvas, 91.4 x 91.4
Courtesy Annely Juda Fine Art

Chance Order Change 18 (4 colours) 1981
oil on canvas, 91.4 x 91.4
Courtesy Annely Juda Fine Art

Chance Order Change 25 (4 colours) History Painting B
1982
oil on canvas, 91.4 x 91.4
Courtesy Annely Juda Fine Art

Four History Pictures 1982
a set of 4 screenprints: A, B, C, D
edition of 90, paper size 84 x 59.2, image size 49 x 49
Courtesy Annely Juda Fine Art

*Chance Order Change 26
(black) History Painting* 1983
oil on canvas
Private Collection

BRIDGET RILEY

Born in London 1931. Brought up in Cornwall and Lincolnshire. Studied at Goldsmiths' School of Art and Royal College of Art. Awarded CBE 1972. Appointed Trustee of the National Gallery 1981. Has exhibited widely throughout the world. Lives and works in London. Represented by the Mayor Rowan Gallery, London.

Descending 1965-6
emulsion on board, 91.5 x 91.5
Private Collection, London

Cornflower 1982
oil on linen, 175.3 x 144.8
Courtesy Mayor Rowan Gallery

Isfahan 1984
oil on linen, 167.4 x 140
Courtesy Mayor Rowan Gallery

Out of the Blue (little zig) 1986
lascaux acrylic on linen, 172.1 x 161.3
Courtesy Mayor Rowan Gallery

Fleeting Moment 1986
oil on linen, 160 x 153
Courtesy Mayor Rowan Gallery

Ease 1987
oil on linen, 161.9 x 158.1
Courtesy Mayor Rowan Gallery

Untitled 1988
oil on linen, 162.6 x 226.1
Courtesy Mayor Rowan Gallery

References are given in the order in which the quoted texts appear in *NOTES AND VOICES*

Adrian Stokes *Colour and Form* (Faber and Faber, London 1937)

Piet Mondrian *Unpublished Notes on Nature and Art, 1938-1943* ed. Harry Holtzman, in THE STRUCTURIST (University of Saskatchewan) No. 23/24 1983/84

D.H. Lawrence *Morality and the Novel* (1925) in PHOENIX (Heinemann, London 1936)

Ludwig Wittgenstein *Tractatus Logico-Philosophicus* (Routledge and Kegan Paul, London 1922) this is part of proposition 6.4311

Paul Klee *On Modern Art* (1924) trans. Paul Findlay (Faber and Faber, London 1948)

Gaston Bachelard *The Poetics of Space* 1958 trans. Maria Jolas (Beacon Press, Boston 1969)

Paul Cézanne from a letter written from Aix to his son Paul, September 8th 1906. (Cézanne died six weeks later.) in CEZANNE BY HIMSELF ed. Richard Kendall (Macdonald, London 1988)

Ludwig Wittgenstein *Tractatus Logico-Philosophicus* this is the first proposition

Leo Steinberg *The Eye Is Part of the Mind in* PARTISAN REVIEW VOL.XX No 2 reprinted in REFLECTIONS ON ART ed. Suzanne K. Langer (The John Hopkins Press New York 1958)

Suzanne K. Langer *Problems of Art: Ten Philosophical Lectures* (Routledge and Kegan Paul, London 1957) see especially 5. *Artistic Perception and "Natural Light"*

William Blake from a letter to the Revd. Dr. Trusler August 23rd 1799

Mark Tobey statements from the catalogue to an exhibition on the occasion of his 80th birthday, Galerie Beyeler, Basel Dec 1970-Feb 1971

Naum Gabo *Art and Science* 1956 in THE NEW LANDSCAPE IN ART AND SCIENCE Gyorgy Kepes (Paul Theobald, Chicago 1956)

KENNETH MARTIN

The passages in the Kenneth Martin text are drawn from the following sources (references in brackets indicate publication):

1 Chance and Order *The Sixth William Townsend Lecture* (Waddington Gallery 1979)

2 Movement and Expression 1966 (DATA 1968)

3 Address to International Conference, Verucchio, Italy 1965 (*Kenneth Martin* Tate Gallery 1975)

4 On Construction (The University of East Anglia Collection UEA 1984)

5 Architecture, Machine and Mobile 1955 (Tate 1975)

6 Townsend Lecture

7 Means and Content 1964 (*Kenneth Martin* Yale Centre for British Art 1979)

8 Townsend Lecture

9 Construction from Within 1964 (*Structure* Amsterdam 1964)

10 Townsend Lecture

11 from unpublished draft for Construction from Within 1964 (see 9 above) (Tate 1975)

12 Construction from Within 1964 (Amsterdam 1964)

13 Townsend Lecture

14 from taped conversation with Alastair Grieve 1984 (*Kenneth Martin The Late Paintings* Serpentine Gallery/Arts Council of Great Britain 1985)

15 Address at Verucchio 1965 (Tate 1975)

TOUR

Newcastle upon Tyne, Laing Art Gallery *27 January – 19 March 1989*
Sheffield, Mappin Art Gallery *1 April – 15 May*
Stoke, City Art Gallery *3 June – 16 July*

CATALOGUE

Not all catalogued works will be shown at each gallery.
Measurements are given in centimetres, height before width.

exhibition organised by Mike Collier and Michael Harrison
assisted by Fiona Chambers and Christine Taylor

catalogue designed by Tamar Burchill
photographs by Martin Charles (cover and p9), David Dilley (pp 21, 33, 51),
Christopher Gallagher (p27), Margaret Mellis (p15), George Meyrick (pp 16, 17, 28, 29, 39, 40, 41)
Anthea Seiveking (p45), Eileen Tweedy, (pp22, 23)
Rodney Todd-White (pp 34, 35)
John Webb (pp 52, 53)

printed by Elwick Grover Aicken Partners, Brighton

© The South Bank Centre 1989
ISBN 1 85332 036 6

a full list of South Bank Centre publications
may be obtained from:

The Publications Office
South Bank Centre
Royal Festival Hall
Belvedere Road
London SE1 8XX

Front cover Gillian Ayres' studio, Wales, 1987
Back cover James Hugonin